THIS BOOK BELONGS TO

HOW TO USE

This Log Book contains an individual page for each Munro with space to fill out the details of your personal climbs.

You will also see the symbol below against some of the Munro's which signifies that these Munro's are suitable for beginners.

A' BHUIDHEANACH BHEAG

LOCATION
Cairngorms

HEIGHT
936 Metres
3071 Feet

DATE CLIMBED

ENJOYABLE
☆ ☆ ☆

ROUTE

CONDITION

NOTES

A' CHAILLEACH

LOCATION
Ullapool

HEIGHT
997 Metres
3271 Feet

DATE CLIMBED

ENJOYABLE
☆ ☆ ☆

ROUTE

CONDITION

NOTES

A' CHAILLEACH (MONADHLIATH)

LOCATION
Cairngorms

HEIGHT
930 Metres
3051 Feet

DATE CLIMBED

ENJOYABLE
☆ ☆ ☆

ROUTE

CONDITION

NOTES

A' CHRALAIG

LOCATION
Kintail

HEIGHT
1120 Metres
3674 Feet

DATE CLIMBED

ENJOYABLE
☆ ☆ ☆

ROUTE

CONDITION

NOTES

A' GHLAS-BHEINN

LOCATION
Kintail

HEIGHT
918 Metres
3011 Feet

DATE CLIMBED

ENJOYABLE
☆☆☆

ROUTE

CONDITION

NOTES

A' MHAIGHDEAN

LOCATION
Ullapool

HEIGHT
967 Metres
3172 Feet

DATE CLIMBED

ENJOYABLE
☆ ☆ ☆

ROUTE

CONDITION

NOTES

A' MHARCONAICH

LOCATION
Cairngorms

HEIGHT
975 Metres
3198 Feet

DATE CLIMBED

ENJOYABLE
☆ ☆ ☆

ROUTE

CONDITION

NOTES

AM BASTEIR

LOCATION
Islands

HEIGHT
934 Metres
3064 Feet

DATE CLIMBED

ENJOYABLE
☆ ☆ ☆

ROUTE

CONDITION

NOTES

AM BODACH

LOCATION
Fort William

HEIGHT
1032 Metres
3385 Feet

DATE CLIMBED
_____

ENJOYABLE
☆ ☆ ☆

ROUTE
_____

CONDITION
_____

NOTES
_____
_____
_____

AM FAOCHAGACH

LOCATION
Ullapool

HEIGHT
954 Metres
3129 Feet

DATE CLIMBED

ENJOYABLE
☆ ☆ ☆

ROUTE

CONDITION

NOTES

AN CAISTEAL

LOCATION
Loch Lomond

HEIGHT
995 Metres
3264 Feet

DATE CLIMBED

ENJOYABLE
☆ ☆ ☆

ROUTE

CONDITION

NOTES

AN COILEACHAN

LOCATION
Ullapool

HEIGHT
923 Metres
3028 Feet

DATE CLIMBED

ENJOYABLE
☆ ☆ ☆

ROUTE

CONDITION

NOTES

AN GEARANACH

LOCATION
Fort William

HEIGHT
982 Metres
3221 Feet

DATE CLIMBED

ENJOYABLE
☆ ☆ ☆

ROUTE

CONDITION

NOTES

AN RIABHACHAN

LOCATION
Loch Ness

HEIGHT
1129 Metres
3704 Feet

DATE CLIMBED

ENJOYABLE
☆ ☆ ☆

ROUTE

CONDITION

NOTES

15

AN SGARSOCH

LOCATION
Cairngorms

HEIGHT
1006 Metres
3300 Feet

DATE CLIMBED

ENJOYABLE
☆ ☆ ☆

ROUTE

CONDITION

NOTES

AN SOCACH (AFFRIC)

LOCATION

Loch Ness

HEIGHT

921 Metres
3021 Feet

DATE CLIMBED

ENJOYABLE

☆ ☆ ☆

ROUTE

CONDITION

NOTES

AN SOCACH (BRAEMAR)

LOCATION
Cairngorms

HEIGHT
944 Metres
3097 Feet

DATE CLIMBED

ENJOYABLE
☆☆☆

ROUTE

CONDITION

NOTES

AN SOCACH (MULLARDOCH)

LOCATION

Loch Ness

HEIGHT

1069 Metres
3507 Feet

DATE CLIMBED

_____

ENJOYABLE

☆ ☆ ☆

ROUTE

_____

CONDITION

_____

NOTES

_____
_____
_____

AN STUC

LOCATION
Perthshire

HEIGHT
1118 Metres
3667 Feet

DATE CLIMBED
19/11/22

ENJOYABLE
★☆☆

ROUTE

CONDITION

NOTES

AONACH AIR CHRITH

LOCATION
Kintail

HEIGHT
1021 Metres
3349 Feet

DATE CLIMBED
_____

ENJOYABLE
☆ ☆ ☆

ROUTE
_____

CONDITION
_____

NOTES
_____
_____
_____

AONACH BEAG (ALDER)

LOCATION
Cairngorms

HEIGHT
1116 Metres
3661 Feet

DATE CLIMBED

ENJOYABLE
☆ ☆ ☆

ROUTE

CONDITION

NOTES

AONACH BEAG (NEVIS RANGE)

LOCATION
Fort William

HEIGHT
1234 Metres
4048 Feet

DATE CLIMBED

ENJOYABLE
☆ ☆ ☆

ROUTE

CONDITION

NOTES

AONACH MEADHOIN

LOCATION
Kintail

HEIGHT
1001 Metres
3284 Feet

DATE CLIMBED

ENJOYABLE
☆ ☆ ☆

ROUTE

CONDITION

NOTES

AONACH MOR

LOCATION
Fort William

HEIGHT
221 Metres
4005 Feet

DATE CLIMBED

ENJOYABLE
☆ ☆ ☆

ROUTE

CONDITION

NOTES

BEINN A'BHUIRD

LOCATION
Cairngorms

HEIGHT
1197 Metres
3927 Feet

DATE CLIMBED

ENJOYABLE
☆ ☆ ☆

ROUTE

CONDITION

NOTES

BEINN A'CHAORAINN (CAIRNGORMS)

LOCATION

Cairngorms

HEIGHT

1082 Metres
3549 Feet

DATE CLIMBED

ENJOYABLE

☆ ☆ ☆

ROUTE

CONDITION

NOTES

BEINN A'CHAORAINN (GLEN SPEAN)

LOCATION
Fort William

HEIGHT
1050 Metres
3444 Feet

DATE CLIMBED

ENJOYABLE
☆☆☆

ROUTE

CONDITION

NOTES

BEINN A'CHLACHAIR

LOCATION
Fort William

HEIGHT
1087 Metres
3566 Feet

DATE CLIMBED

ENJOYABLE
☆ ☆ ☆

ROUTE

CONDITION

NOTES

BEINN A'CHLEIBH

LOCATION
Argyll

HEIGHT
916 Metres
3005 Feet

DATE CLIMBED

ENJOYABLE
☆ ☆ ☆

ROUTE

CONDITION

NOTES

BEINN A'CHOCHUILL

LOCATION

Argyll

HEIGHT

980 Metres
3215 Feet

DATE CLIMBED

ENJOYABLE

☆ ☆ ☆

ROUTE

CONDITION

NOTES

BEINN A'CHREACHAIN

LOCATION
Argyll

HEIGHT
1081 Metres
3546 Feet

DATE CLIMBED

ENJOYABLE
☆ ☆ ☆

ROUTE

CONDITION

NOTES

BEINN A'CHROIN

LOCATION
Loch Lomond

HEIGHT
942 Metres
3090 Feet

DATE CLIMBED

ENJOYABLE
☆ ☆ ☆

ROUTE

CONDITION

NOTES

BEINN ACHALADAIR

LOCATION
Argyll

HEIGHT
1038 Metres
3405 Feet

DATE CLIMBED
_____

ENJOYABLE
☆ ☆ ☆

ROUTE
_____

CONDITION
_____

NOTES
_____
_____
_____

BEINN AN DOTHAIDH

LOCATION
Argyll

HEIGHT
1004 Metres
3293 Feet

DATE CLIMBED

ENJOYABLE
☆ ☆ ☆

ROUTE

CONDITION

NOTES

BEINN BHEOIL

LOCATION

Cairngorms

HEIGHT

1019 Metres
3343 Feet

DATE CLIMBED

ENJOYABLE

☆ ☆ ☆

ROUTE

CONDITION

NOTES

BEINN BHREAC

LOCATION

Cairngorms

HEIGHT

931 Metres
3054 Feet

DATE CLIMBED

_____

ENJOYABLE

☆ ☆ ☆

ROUTE

_____

CONDITION

_____

NOTES

_____
_____
_____

BEINN BHROTAIN

LOCATION
Cairngorms

HEIGHT
1157 Metres
3795 Feet

DATE CLIMBED

ENJOYABLE
☆ ☆ ☆

ROUTE

CONDITION

NOTES

BEINN BHUIDHE

LOCATION
Argyll

HEIGHT
948 Metres
3110 Feet

DATE CLIMBED

ENJOYABLE
☆ ☆ ☆

ROUTE

CONDITION

NOTES

BEINN CHABHAIR

LOCATION
Loch Lomond

HEIGHT
933 Metres
3061 Feet

DATE CLIMBED

ENJOYABLE
☆ ☆ ☆

ROUTE

CONDITION

NOTES

BEINN DEARG (BLAIR ATHOLL)

LOCATION
Perthshire

HEIGHT
1008 Metres
3307 Feet

DATE CLIMBED

ENJOYABLE
☆ ☆ ☆

ROUTE

CONDITION

NOTES

BEINN DEARG (ULLAPOOL)

LOCATION
Ullapool

HEIGHT
1084 Metres
3556 Feet

DATE CLIMBED

ENJOYABLE
☆ ☆ ☆

ROUTE

CONDITION

NOTES

BEINN DORAIN

LOCATION
Argyll

HEIGHT
1076 Metres
3530 Feet

DATE CLIMBED

ENJOYABLE
☆ ☆ ☆

ROUTE

CONDITION

NOTES

BEINN DUBHCHRAIG

LOCATION
Argyll

HEIGHT
978 Metres
3208 Feet

DATE CLIMBED

ENJOYABLE
☆ ☆ ☆

ROUTE

CONDITION

NOTES

BEINN EIBHINN

LOCATION
Cairngorms

HEIGHT
1102 Metres
3615 Feet

DATE CLIMBED
_____

ENJOYABLE
☆ ☆ ☆

ROUTE
_____

CONDITION
_____

NOTES
_____
_____
_____

BEINN EUNAICH

LOCATION
Argyll

HEIGHT
989 Metres
3244 Feet

DATE CLIMBED

ENJOYABLE
☆ ☆ ☆

ROUTE

CONDITION

NOTES

BEINN FHADA

LOCATION
Kintail

HEIGHT
1032 Metres
3385 Feet

DATE CLIMBED

ENJOYABLE
☆ ☆ ☆

ROUTE

CONDITION

NOTES

BEINN FHIONNLAIDH

LOCATION
Argyll

HEIGHT
959 Metres
3146 Feet

DATE CLIMBED

ENJOYABLE
☆ ☆ ☆

ROUTE

CONDITION

NOTES

BEINN FHIONNLAIDH (CARN EIGE)

LOCATION
Loch Ness

HEIGHT
1005 Metres
3297 Feet

DATE CLIMBED

ENJOYABLE
☆☆☆

ROUTE

CONDITION

NOTES

BEINN GHLAS

LOCATION
Perthshire

HEIGHT
1103 Metres
3618 Feet

DATE CLIMBED

ENJOYABLE
☆☆☆

ROUTE

CONDITION

NOTES

BEINN HEASGARNICH

LOCATION
Perthshire

HEIGHT
1078 Metres
3536 Feet

DATE CLIMBED
_____

ENJOYABLE
☆ ☆ ☆

ROUTE
_____

CONDITION
_____

NOTES
_____
_____
_____

BEINN IME

LOCATION
Loch Lomond

HEIGHT
1011 Metres
3316 Feet

DATE CLIMBED

ENJOYABLE
☆ ☆ ☆

ROUTE

CONDITION

NOTES

BEINN IUTHARN MHOR

LOCATION
Cairngorms

HEIGHT
1045 Metres
3428 Feet

DATE CLIMBED

ENJOYABLE
☆ ☆ ☆

ROUTE

CONDITION

NOTES

BEINN LIATH MHOR

LOCATION
Torridon

HEIGHT
926 Metres
3038 Feet

DATE CLIMBED

ENJOYABLE
☆ ☆ ☆

ROUTE

CONDITION

NOTES

BEINN LIATH MHOR FANNAICH

LOCATION
Ullapool

HEIGHT
954 Metres
3129 Feet

DATE CLIMBED

ENJOYABLE
☆☆☆

ROUTE

CONDITION

NOTES

BEINN MHANACH

LOCATION
Argyll

HEIGHT
953 Metres
3126 Feet

DATE CLIMBED

ENJOYABLE
☆ ☆ ☆

ROUTE

CONDITION

NOTES

BEINN MHEADHOIN

LOCATION

Cairngorms

HEIGHT

1182 Metres
3877 Feet

DATE CLIMBED

_____

ENJOYABLE

☆ ☆ ☆

ROUTE

_____

CONDITION

_____

NOTES

_____
_____
_____

BEINN NA LAP

LOCATION

Fort William

HEIGHT

937 Metres
3074 Feet

DATE CLIMBED

ENJOYABLE

☆ ☆ ☆

ROUTE

CONDITION

NOTES

BEINN NAN AIGHENAN

LOCATION
Fort William

HEIGHT
960 Metres
3149 Feet

DATE CLIMBED

ENJOYABLE
☆ ☆ ☆

ROUTE

CONDITION

NOTES

BEINN NARNAIN

LOCATION
Loch Lomond

HEIGHT
926 Metres
3038 Feet

DATE CLIMBED

ENJOYABLE
☆ ☆ ☆

ROUTE

CONDITION

NOTES

BEINN SGRITHEALL

LOCATION
Kintail

HEIGHT
974 Metres
3195 Feet

DATE CLIMBED

ENJOYABLE
☆ ☆ ☆

ROUTE

CONDITION

NOTES

BEINN SGULAIRD

LOCATION

Argyll

HEIGHT

937 Metres
3074 Feet

DATE CLIMBED

ENJOYABLE

☆ ☆ ☆

ROUTE

CONDITION

NOTES

BEINN TARSUINN

LOCATION
Ullapool

HEIGHT
937 Metres
3074 Feet

DATE CLIMBED
_____

ENJOYABLE
☆ ☆ ☆

ROUTE
_____

CONDITION
_____

NOTES
_____
_____
_____

BEINN TEALLACH

LOCATION
Fort William

HEIGHT
915 Metres
3001 Feet

DATE CLIMBED

ENJOYABLE
☆ ☆ ☆

ROUTE

CONDITION

NOTES

BEINN TULAICHEAN

LOCATION
Loch Lomond

HEIGHT
946 Metres
3103 Feet

DATE CLIMBED

ENJOYABLE
☆ ☆ ☆

ROUTE

CONDITION

NOTES

BEINN UDLAMAIN

LOCATION
Cairngorms

HEIGHT
1010 Metres
3313 Feet

DATE CLIMBED

ENJOYABLE
☆ ☆ ☆

ROUTE

CONDITION

NOTES

BEN ALDER

LOCATION
Cairngorms

HEIGHT
1148 Metres
3766 Feet

DATE CLIMBED

ENJOYABLE
☆☆☆

ROUTE

CONDITION

NOTES

BEN AVON

LOCATION
Cairngorms

HEIGHT
1171 Metres
3841 Feet

DATE CLIMBED

ENJOYABLE
☆ ☆ ☆

ROUTE

CONDITION

NOTES

BEN CHALLUM

LOCATION
Argyll

HEIGHT
1025 Metres
3362 Feet

DATE CLIMBED

ENJOYABLE
☆ ☆ ☆

ROUTE

CONDITION

NOTES

BEN CHONZIE

LOCATION
Perthshire

HEIGHT
931 Metres
3054 Feet

DATE CLIMBED

ENJOYABLE
☆ ☆ ☆

ROUTE

CONDITION

NOTES

BEN CRUACHAN

LOCATION
Argyll

HEIGHT
1126 Metres
3694 Feet

DATE CLIMBED

ENJOYABLE
☆ ☆ ☆

ROUTE

CONDITION

NOTES

BEN HOPE

LOCATION
Sutherland

HEIGHT
927 Metres
3041 Feet

DATE CLIMBED

ENJOYABLE
☆☆☆

ROUTE

CONDITION

NOTES

BEN KLIBRECK

LOCATION
Sutherland

HEIGHT
961 Metres
3152 Feet

DATE CLIMBED
_____

ENJOYABLE
☆ ☆ ☆

ROUTE
_____

CONDITION
_____

NOTES
_____
_____
_____

BEN LAWERS

LOCATION
Perthshire

HEIGHT
1214 Metres
3982 Feet

DATE CLIMBED

ENJOYABLE
☆ ☆ ☆

ROUTE

CONDITION

NOTES

BEN LOMOND

LOCATION
Loch Lomond

HEIGHT
974 Metres
3195 Feet

DATE CLIMBED

ENJOYABLE
☆ ☆ ☆

ROUTE

CONDITION

NOTES

BEN LUI

LOCATION
Argyll

HEIGHT
1130 Metres
3707 Feet

DATE CLIMBED

ENJOYABLE
☆☆☆

ROUTE

CONDITION

NOTES

BEN MACDUI

LOCATION
Cairngorms

HEIGHT
1309 Metres
4294 Feet

DATE CLIMBED

ENJOYABLE
☆ ☆ ☆

ROUTE

CONDITION

NOTES

BEN MORE

LOCATION
Loch Lomond

HEIGHT
1174 Metres
3851 Feet

DATE CLIMBED

ENJOYABLE
☆ ☆ ☆

ROUTE

CONDITION

NOTES

BEN MORE (MULL)

LOCATION
Islands

HEIGHT
966 Metres
3169 Feet

DATE CLIMBED
_____

ENJOYABLE
☆ ☆ ☆

ROUTE
_____

CONDITION
_____

NOTES
_____
_____
_____

BEN MORE ASSYNT

LOCATION

Ullapool

HEIGHT

998 Metres
3274 Feet

DATE CLIMBED

ENJOYABLE

☆☆☆

ROUTE

CONDITION

NOTES

BEN NEVIS

LOCATION
Fort William

HEIGHT
1345 Metres
4412 Feet

DATE CLIMBED
_____

ENJOYABLE
☆ ☆ ☆

ROUTE
_____

CONDITION
_____

NOTES
_____
_____
_____

BEN OSS

LOCATION
Argyll

HEIGHT
1029 Metres
3375 Feet

DATE CLIMBED

ENJOYABLE
☆ ☆ ☆

ROUTE

CONDITION

NOTES

BEN STARAV

LOCATION
Fort William

HEIGHT
1078 Metres
3536 Feet

DATE CLIMBED

ENJOYABLE
☆ ☆ ☆

ROUTE

CONDITION

NOTES

BEN VANE

LOCATION
Loch Lomond

HEIGHT
915 Metres
3001 Feet

DATE CLIMBED

ENJOYABLE
☆ ☆ ☆

ROUTE

CONDITION

NOTES

BEN VORLICH (LOCH EARN)

LOCATION
Perthshire

HEIGHT
985 Metres
3231 Feet

DATE CLIMBED

ENJOYABLE
☆ ☆ ☆

ROUTE

CONDITION

NOTES

BEN VORLICH (LOCH LOMOND)

LOCATION
Loch Lomond

HEIGHT
943 Metres
3093 Feet

DATE CLIMBED

ENJOYABLE
☆ ☆ ☆

ROUTE

CONDITION

NOTES

BEN WYVIS

LOCATION
Loch Ness

HEIGHT
1046 Metres
3431 Feet

DATE CLIMBED

ENJOYABLE

ROUTE

CONDITION

NOTES

BIDEAN NAM BIAN

LOCATION

Fort William

HEIGHT

1150 Metres
3772 Feet

DATE CLIMBED

ENJOYABLE

☆ ☆ ☆

ROUTE

CONDITION

NOTES

BIDEIN A'CHOIRE SHEASGAICH

LOCATION

Torridon

HEIGHT

945 Metres
3100 Feet

DATE CLIMBED

ENJOYABLE

☆☆☆

ROUTE

CONDITION

NOTES

89

BIDEIN A'GHLAS THUILL (AN TEALLACH)

LOCATION
Ullapool

HEIGHT
1062 Metres
3484 Feet

DATE CLIMBED

ENJOYABLE
☆ ☆ ☆

ROUTE

CONDITION

NOTES

BINNEIN BEAG

LOCATION
Fort William

HEIGHT
943 Metres
3093 Feet

DATE CLIMBED

ENJOYABLE
☆ ☆ ☆

ROUTE

CONDITION

NOTES

BINNEIN MOR

LOCATION
Fort William

HEIGHT
1130 Metres
3707 Feet

DATE CLIMBED

ENJOYABLE
☆ ☆ ☆

ROUTE

CONDITION

NOTES

BLA BHEINN

LOCATION
Islands

HEIGHT
928 Metres
3044 Feet

DATE CLIMBED
_____

ENJOYABLE
☆ ☆ ☆

ROUTE
_____

CONDITION
_____

NOTES
_____
_____
_____

BRAERIACH

LOCATION

Cairngorms

HEIGHT

1296 Metres
4251 Feet

DATE CLIMBED

ENJOYABLE

☆ ☆ ☆

ROUTE

CONDITION

NOTES

BRAIGH COIRE CHRUINN-BHALGAIN

LOCATION
Perthshire

HEIGHT
1070 Metres
3510 Feet

DATE CLIMBED

ENJOYABLE
☆ ☆ ☆

ROUTE

CONDITION

NOTES

BROAD CAIRN

LOCATION
Cairngorms

HEIGHT
998 Metres
3274 Feet

DATE CLIMBED

ENJOYABLE
☆ ☆ ☆

ROUTE

CONDITION

NOTES

BRUACH NA FRITHE

LOCATION

Islands

HEIGHT

958 Metres
3143 Feet

DATE CLIMBED

_____

ENJOYABLE

☆ ☆ ☆

ROUTE

_____

CONDITION

_____

NOTES

_____
_____
_____

BYNACK MORE

LOCATION
Cairngorms

HEIGHT
1090 Metres
3576 Feet

DATE CLIMBED

ENJOYABLE
☆ ☆ ☆

ROUTE

CONDITION

NOTES

CAIRN BANNOCH

LOCATION
Cairngorms

HEIGHT
1012 Metres
3320 Feet

DATE CLIMBED

ENJOYABLE
☆ ☆ ☆

ROUTE

CONDITION

NOTES

CAIRN GORM

LOCATION
Cairngorms

HEIGHT
1245 Metres
4084 Feet

DATE CLIMBED

ENJOYABLE
☆ ☆ ☆

ROUTE

CONDITION

NOTES

CAIRN OF CLAISE

LOCATION
Cairngorms

HEIGHT
1064 Metres
3490 Feet

DATE CLIMBED

ENJOYABLE
☆ ☆ ☆

ROUTE

CONDITION

NOTES

CAIRN TOUL

LOCATION
Cairngorms

HEIGHT
1291 Metres
4235 Feet

DATE CLIMBED

ENJOYABLE
☆ ☆ ☆

ROUTE

CONDITION

NOTES

CARN A'CHLAMAIN

LOCATION
Perthshire

HEIGHT
963 Metres
3159 Feet

DATE CLIMBED

ENJOYABLE
☆☆☆

ROUTE

CONDITION

NOTES

CARN A'CHOIRE BHOIDHEACH

LOCATION
Cairngorms

HEIGHT
1118 Metres
3667 Feet

DATE CLIMBED

ENJOYABLE
☆ ☆ ☆

ROUTE

CONDITION

NOTES

CARN A'GHEOIDH

LOCATION
Cairngorms

HEIGHT
975 Metres
3198 Feet

DATE CLIMBED

ENJOYABLE
☆ ☆ ☆

ROUTE

CONDITION

NOTES

CARN A'MHAIM

LOCATION

Cairngorms

HEIGHT

1037 Metres
3402 Feet

DATE CLIMBED

ENJOYABLE

☆ ☆ ☆

ROUTE

CONDITION

NOTES

CARN AN FHIDHLEIR (CARN EALAR)

LOCATION
Cairngorms

HEIGHT
994 Metres
3261 Feet

DATE CLIMBED

ENJOYABLE
☆ ☆ ☆

ROUTE

CONDITION

NOTES

CARN AN RIGH

LOCATION
Perthshire

HEIGHT
1029 Metres
3375 Feet

DATE CLIMBED

ENJOYABLE
☆☆☆

ROUTE

CONDITION

NOTES

CARN AN T-SAGAIRT MOR

LOCATION
Cairngorms

HEIGHT
1047 Metres
3435 Feet

DATE CLIMBED

ENJOYABLE
☆ ☆ ☆

ROUTE

CONDITION

NOTES

109

CARN AN TUIRC

LOCATION
Cairngorms

HEIGHT
1019 Metres
3343 Feet

DATE CLIMBED
2/1/2023

ENJOYABLE
★★★

ROUTE
WALK HIGHLADS

CONDITION
WINTER

NOTES
WITH LISA. CRAMPONS ON MOST OF DAY

CARN AOSDA

LOCATION
Cairngorms

HEIGHT
917 Metres
3008 Feet

DATE CLIMBED
23/9/20

ENJOYABLE
★✓ ★✓ ★✓

ROUTE

CONDITION
SUMMER

NOTES
WITH LISA.

CARN BHAC

LOCATION
Cairngorms

HEIGHT
946 Metres
3103 Feet

DATE CLIMBED

ENJOYABLE
☆ ☆ ☆

ROUTE

CONDITION

NOTES

CARN DEARG (CORROUR)

LOCATION
Fort William

HEIGHT
941 Metres
3087 Feet

DATE CLIMBED

ENJOYABLE
☆ ☆ ☆

ROUTE

CONDITION

NOTES

CARN DEARG (LOCH PATTACK)

LOCATION
Cairngorms

HEIGHT
1034 Metres
3392 Feet

DATE CLIMBED

ENJOYABLE
☆ ☆ ☆

ROUTE

CONDITION

NOTES

CARN DEARG (MONADHLIATH)

LOCATION
Cairngorms

HEIGHT
945 Metres
3100 Feet

DATE CLIMBED

ENJOYABLE
☆ ☆ ☆

ROUTE

CONDITION

NOTES

CARN EIGE

LOCATION

Loch Ness

HEIGHT

1183 Metres
3881 Feet

DATE CLIMBED

ENJOYABLE

☆ ☆ ☆

ROUTE

CONDITION

NOTES

CARN GHLUASAID

LOCATION
Kintail

HEIGHT
957 Metres
3139 Feet

DATE CLIMBED
_____

ENJOYABLE
☆ ☆ ☆

ROUTE
_____

CONDITION
_____

NOTES
_____
_____
_____

CARN GORM

LOCATION
Perthshire

HEIGHT
1029 Metres
3375 Feet

DATE CLIMBED

ENJOYABLE
☆ ☆ ☆

ROUTE

CONDITION

NOTES

CARN LIATH (BEINN A'GHLO)

LOCATION
Perthshire

HEIGHT
975 Metres
3198 Feet

DATE CLIMBED

ENJOYABLE
☆ ☆ ☆

ROUTE

CONDITION

NOTES

CARN LIATH (CREAG MEAGAIDH)

LOCATION
Fort William

HEIGHT
1006 Metres
3300 Feet

DATE CLIMBED

ENJOYABLE
☆ ☆ ☆

ROUTE

CONDITION

NOTES

CARN MAIRG

LOCATION
Perthshire

HEIGHT
1042 Metres
3418 Feet

DATE CLIMBED

ENJOYABLE
☆ ☆ ☆

ROUTE

CONDITION

NOTES

CARN MOR DEARG

LOCATION
Fort William

HEIGHT
1220 Metres
4002 Feet

DATE CLIMBED

ENJOYABLE
☆ ☆ ☆

ROUTE

CONDITION

NOTES

CARN NA CAIM

LOCATION
Cairngorms

HEIGHT
941 Metres
3087 Feet

DATE CLIMBED

ENJOYABLE
☆☆☆

ROUTE

CONDITION

NOTES

CARN NAN GABHAR

LOCATION
Perthshire

HEIGHT
1121 Metres
3677 Feet

DATE CLIMBED

ENJOYABLE
☆ ☆ ☆

ROUTE

CONDITION

NOTES

CARN NAN GOBHAR (LOCH MULLARDOCH)

LOCATION
Loch Ness

HEIGHT
992 Metres
3254 Feet

DATE CLIMBED

ENJOYABLE
☆ ☆ ☆

ROUTE

CONDITION

NOTES

CARN NAN GOBHAR (STRATHFARRAR)

LOCATION
Loch Ness

HEIGHT
992 Metres
3254 Feet

DATE CLIMBED

ENJOYABLE
☆ ☆ ☆

ROUTE

CONDITION

NOTES

CARN SGULAIN

LOCATION

Cairngorms

HEIGHT

920 Metres
3018 Feet

DATE CLIMBED

ENJOYABLE

☆ ☆ ☆

ROUTE

CONDITION

NOTES

CHNO DEARG

LOCATION
Fort William

HEIGHT
1046 Metres
3431 Feet

DATE CLIMBED

ENJOYABLE
☆☆☆

ROUTE

CONDITION

NOTES

CISTE DHUBH

LOCATION
Kintail

HEIGHT
979 Metres
3211 Feet

DATE CLIMBED

ENJOYABLE
☆ ☆ ☆

ROUTE

CONDITION

NOTES

CONA' MHEALL

LOCATION
Ullapool

HEIGHT
978 Metres
3208 Feet

DATE CLIMBED

ENJOYABLE
☆ ☆ ☆

ROUTE

CONDITION

NOTES

CONIVAL

LOCATION
Ullapool

HEIGHT
987 Metres
3238 Feet

DATE CLIMBED

ENJOYABLE
☆ ☆ ☆

ROUTE

CONDITION

NOTES

CREAG A'MHAIM

LOCATION
Kintail

HEIGHT
947 Metres
3106 Feet

DATE CLIMBED

ENJOYABLE
☆ ☆ ☆

ROUTE

CONDITION

NOTES

CREAG LEACACH

LOCATION
Cairngorms

HEIGHT
987 Metres
3238 Feet

DATE CLIMBED

ENJOYABLE
☆☆☆

ROUTE

CONDITION

NOTES

133

CREAG MEAGAIDH

LOCATION
Fort William

HEIGHT
1130 Metres
3707 Feet

DATE CLIMBED

ENJOYABLE
☆ ☆ ☆

ROUTE

CONDITION

NOTES

CREAG MHOR
(GLEN LOCHAY)

LOCATION
Perthshire

HEIGHT
1047 Metres
3435 Feet

DATE CLIMBED

ENJOYABLE
☆ ☆ ☆

ROUTE

CONDITION

NOTES

CREAG MHOR (MEALL NA AIGHEAN)

LOCATION

Perthshire

HEIGHT

981 Metres
3218 Feet

DATE CLIMBED

_____

ENJOYABLE

☆ ☆ ☆

ROUTE

_____

CONDITION

_____

NOTES

_____
_____
_____

CREAG NAN DAMH

LOCATION
Kintail

HEIGHT
918 Metres
3011 Feet

DATE CLIMBED

ENJOYABLE

☆ ☆ ☆

ROUTE

CONDITION

NOTES

CREAG PITRIDH

LOCATION
Fort William

HEIGHT
924 Metres
3031 Feet

DATE CLIMBED

ENJOYABLE
☆ ☆ ☆

ROUTE

CONDITION

NOTES

CREISE

LOCATION
Fort William

HEIGHT
1100 Metres
3608 Feet

DATE CLIMBED

ENJOYABLE
☆ ☆ ☆

ROUTE

CONDITION

NOTES

CRUACH ARDRAIN

LOCATION
Loch Lomond

HEIGHT
1046 Metres
3431 Feet

DATE CLIMBED

ENJOYABLE
☆ ☆ ☆

ROUTE

CONDITION

NOTES

DERRY CAIRNGORM

LOCATION
Cairngorms

HEIGHT
1155 Metres
3789 Feet

DATE CLIMBED

ENJOYABLE
☆ ☆ ☆

ROUTE

CONDITION

NOTES

DRIESH

LOCATION
Angus

HEIGHT
947 Metres
3106 Feet

DATE CLIMBED

ENJOYABLE
☆ ☆ ☆

ROUTE

CONDITION

NOTES

DRUIM SHIONNACH

LOCATION
Kintail

HEIGHT
987 Metres
3238 Feet

DATE CLIMBED

ENJOYABLE
☆ ☆ ☆

ROUTE

CONDITION

NOTES

EIDIDH NAN CLACH GEALA

LOCATION
Ullapool

HEIGHT
927 Metres
3041 Feet

DATE CLIMBED

ENJOYABLE
☆ ☆ ☆

ROUTE

CONDITION

NOTES

FIONN BHEINN

LOCATION
Torridon

HEIGHT
933 Metres
3061 Feet

DATE CLIMBED
_____

ENJOYABLE
☆ ☆ ☆

ROUTE
_____

CONDITION
_____

NOTES
_____
_____
_____

GAIRICH

LOCATION
Fort William

HEIGHT
919 Metres
3015 Feet

DATE CLIMBED

ENJOYABLE
☆ ☆ ☆

ROUTE

CONDITION

NOTES

GARBH CHIOCH MHOR

LOCATION
Fort William

HEIGHT
1013 Metres
3323 Feet

DATE CLIMBED

ENJOYABLE
☆ ☆ ☆

ROUTE

CONDITION

NOTES

GEAL CHARN

LOCATION
Fort William

HEIGHT
1049 Metres
3441 Feet

DATE CLIMBED

ENJOYABLE
☆ ☆ ☆

ROUTE

CONDITION

NOTES

GEAL CHARN (MONADHLIATH)

LOCATION
Cairngorms

HEIGHT
926 Metres
3038 Feet

DATE CLIMBED

ENJOYABLE
☆☆☆

ROUTE

CONDITION

NOTES

GEAL-CHARN
(ALDER)

LOCATION
Cairngorms

HEIGHT
1132 Metres
3713 Feet

DATE CLIMBED

ENJOYABLE
☆ ☆ ☆

ROUTE

CONDITION

NOTES

GEAL-CHARN (DRUMOCHTER)

LOCATION

Cairngorms

HEIGHT

917 Metres
3008 Feet

DATE CLIMBED

ENJOYABLE

☆ ☆ ☆

ROUTE

CONDITION

NOTES

GLAS BHEINN MHOR

LOCATION
Fort William

HEIGHT
997 Metres
3271 Feet

DATE CLIMBED

ENJOYABLE
☆☆☆

ROUTE

CONDITION

NOTES

GLAS MAOL

LOCATION
Cairngorms

HEIGHT
1068 Metres
3503 Feet

DATE CLIMBED

ENJOYABLE
☆ ☆ ☆

ROUTE

CONDITION

NOTES

GLAS TULAICHEAN

LOCATION
Perthshire

HEIGHT
1051 Metres
3448 Feet

DATE CLIMBED

ENJOYABLE
☆ ☆ ☆

ROUTE

CONDITION

NOTES

GLEOURAICH

LOCATION
Fort William

HEIGHT
1035 Metres
3395 Feet

DATE CLIMBED

ENJOYABLE
☆ ☆ ☆

ROUTE

CONDITION

NOTES

GULVAIN

LOCATION

Fort William

HEIGHT

987 Metres
3238 Feet

DATE CLIMBED

ENJOYABLE

☆ ☆ ☆

ROUTE

CONDITION

NOTES

INACCESSIBLE PINNACLE

LOCATION
Islands

HEIGHT
986 Metres
3234 Feet

DATE CLIMBED
_____

ENJOYABLE
☆ ☆ ☆

ROUTE
_____

CONDITION
_____

NOTES
_____
_____
_____

LADHAR BHEINN

LOCATION
Fort William

HEIGHT
1020 Metres
3346 Feet

DATE CLIMBED
_____

ENJOYABLE
☆ ☆ ☆

ROUTE
_____

CONDITION
_____

NOTES
_____
_____
_____

LOCHNAGAR

LOCATION
Cairngorms

HEIGHT
1155 Metres
3789 Feet

DATE CLIMBED

ENJOYABLE
☆ ☆ ☆

ROUTE

CONDITION

NOTES

LUINNE BHEINN

LOCATION
Fort William

HEIGHT
939 Metres
3080 Feet

DATE CLIMBED

ENJOYABLE
☆ ☆ ☆

ROUTE

CONDITION

NOTES

LURG MHOR

LOCATION
Torridon

HEIGHT
986 Metres
3234 Feet

DATE CLIMBED

ENJOYABLE
☆ ☆ ☆

ROUTE

CONDITION

NOTES

MAM SODHAIL

LOCATION
Loch Ness

HEIGHT
1181 Metres
3874 Feet

DATE CLIMBED

ENJOYABLE
☆ ☆ ☆

ROUTE

CONDITION

NOTES

MAOILE LUNNDAIDH

LOCATION
Torridon

HEIGHT
1007 Metres
3303 Feet

DATE CLIMBED

ENJOYABLE
☆ ☆ ☆

ROUTE

CONDITION

NOTES

MAOL CHEAN-DEARG

LOCATION
Torridon

HEIGHT
933 Metres
3061 Feet

DATE CLIMBED

ENJOYABLE
☆ ☆ ☆

ROUTE

CONDITION

NOTES

MAOL CHINN-DEARG

LOCATION
Kintail

HEIGHT
981 Metres
3218 Feet

DATE CLIMBED

ENJOYABLE
☆ ☆ ☆

ROUTE

CONDITION

NOTES

MAYAR

LOCATION
Angus

HEIGHT
928 Metres
3044 Feet

DATE CLIMBED

ENJOYABLE
☆ ☆ ☆

ROUTE

CONDITION

NOTES

MEALL A'BHUIRIDH

LOCATION
Fort William

HEIGHT
1108 Metres
3635 Feet

DATE CLIMBED

ENJOYABLE
☆ ☆ ☆

ROUTE

CONDITION

NOTES

MEALL A'CHOIRE LEITH

LOCATION
Perthshire

HEIGHT
926 Metres
3038 Feet

DATE CLIMBED

ENJOYABLE
☆ ☆ ☆

ROUTE

CONDITION

NOTES

MEALL A'CHRASGAIDH

LOCATION
Ullapool

HEIGHT
934 Metres
3064 Feet

DATE CLIMBED

ENJOYABLE
☆ ☆ ☆

ROUTE

CONDITION

NOTES

MEALL BUIDHE (GLEN LYON)

LOCATION
Perthshire

HEIGHT
932 Metres
3057 Feet

DATE CLIMBED

ENJOYABLE
☆☆☆

ROUTE

CONDITION

NOTES

MEALL BUIDHE (KNOYDART)

LOCATION
Fort William

HEIGHT
946 Metres
3103 Feet

DATE CLIMBED

ENJOYABLE
☆ ☆ ☆

ROUTE

CONDITION

NOTES

MEALL CHUAICH

LOCATION

Cairngorms

HEIGHT

951 Metres
3120 Feet

DATE CLIMBED

ENJOYABLE

☆☆☆

ROUTE

CONDITION

NOTES

MEALL CORRANAICH

LOCATION
Perthshire

HEIGHT
1069 Metres
3507 Feet

DATE CLIMBED

ENJOYABLE
☆ ☆ ☆

ROUTE

CONDITION

NOTES

MEALL DEARG (AONACH EAGACH)

LOCATION

Fort William

HEIGHT

953 Metres
3126 Feet

DATE CLIMBED

ENJOYABLE

☆☆☆

ROUTE

CONDITION

NOTES

MEALL GARBH (BEN LAWERS)

LOCATION
Perthshire

HEIGHT
1118 Metres
3667 Feet

DATE CLIMBED
_____

ENJOYABLE
☆ ☆ ☆

ROUTE

_____

CONDITION

_____

NOTES

_____
_____
_____

MEALL GARBH (CARN MAIRG)

LOCATION

Perthshire

HEIGHT

968 Metres
3175 Feet

DATE CLIMBED

ENJOYABLE

☆ ☆ ☆

ROUTE

CONDITION

NOTES

MEALL GHAORDAIDH

LOCATION
Perthshire

HEIGHT
1039 Metres
3408 Feet

DATE CLIMBED

ENJOYABLE
☆ ☆ ☆

ROUTE

CONDITION

NOTES

MEALL GLAS

LOCATION
Loch Lomond

HEIGHT
959 Metres
3146 Feet

DATE CLIMBED

ENJOYABLE
☆☆☆

ROUTE

CONDITION

NOTES

MEALL GORM

LOCATION
Ullapool

HEIGHT
949 Metres
3113 Feet

DATE CLIMBED

ENJOYABLE
☆ ☆ ☆

ROUTE

CONDITION

NOTES

MEALL GREIGH

LOCATION

Perthshire

HEIGHT

1001 Metres
3284 Feet

DATE CLIMBED

ENJOYABLE

☆ ☆ ☆

_____

ROUTE

CONDITION

_____ _____

NOTES

_____
_____
_____

180

MEALL NA TEANGA

LOCATION
Fort William

HEIGHT
918 Metres
3011 Feet

DATE CLIMBED

ENJOYABLE
☆ ☆ ☆

ROUTE

CONDITION

NOTES

MEALL NAN CEAPRAICHEAN

LOCATION
Ullapool

HEIGHT
977 Metres
3205 Feet

DATE CLIMBED

ENJOYABLE
☆ ☆ ☆

ROUTE

CONDITION

NOTES

MEALL NAN EUN

LOCATION
Fort William

HEIGHT
928 Metres
3044 Feet

DATE CLIMBED
_____

ENJOYABLE
☆ ☆ ☆

ROUTE
_____

CONDITION
_____

NOTES
_____
_____
_____

183

MEALL NAN TARMACHAN

LOCATION

Perthshire

HEIGHT

1044 Metres
3425 Feet

DATE CLIMBED

ENJOYABLE

☆ ☆ ☆

ROUTE

CONDITION

NOTES

MONADH MOR

LOCATION
Cairngorms

HEIGHT
1113 Metres
3651 Feet

DATE CLIMBED

ENJOYABLE
☆ ☆ ☆

ROUTE

CONDITION

NOTES

MORUISG

LOCATION
Torridon

HEIGHT
928 Metres
3044 Feet

DATE CLIMBED

ENJOYABLE
☆ ☆ ☆

ROUTE

CONDITION

NOTES

MOUNT KEEN

LOCATION
Angus

HEIGHT
939 Metres
3080 Feet

DATE CLIMBED

ENJOYABLE
☆ ☆ ☆

ROUTE

CONDITION

NOTES

MULLACH AN RATHAIN (LIATHACH)

LOCATION
Torridon

HEIGHT
1023 Metres
3356 Feet

DATE CLIMBED

ENJOYABLE
☆ ☆ ☆

ROUTE

CONDITION

NOTES

MULLACH CLACH A'BHLAIR

LOCATION
Cairngorms

HEIGHT
1019 Metres
3343 Feet

DATE CLIMBED

ENJOYABLE
☆☆☆

ROUTE

CONDITION

NOTES

MULLACH COIRE MHIC FHEARCHAIR

LOCATION
Ullapool

HEIGHT
1019 Metres
3343 Feet

DATE CLIMBED

ENJOYABLE
☆ ☆ ☆

ROUTE

CONDITION

NOTES

MULLACH FRAOCH-CHOIRE

LOCATION
Kintail

HEIGHT
1102 Metres
3615 Feet

DATE CLIMBED

ENJOYABLE
☆ ☆ ☆

ROUTE

CONDITION

NOTES

MULLACH NAN COIREAN

LOCATION
Fort William

HEIGHT
939 Metres
3080 Feet

DATE CLIMBED

ENJOYABLE
☆ ☆ ☆

ROUTE

CONDITION

NOTES

MULLACH NAN DHEIRAGAIN

LOCATION
Loch Ness

HEIGHT
982 Metres
3221 Feet

DATE CLIMBED

ENJOYABLE
☆ ☆ ☆

ROUTE

CONDITION

NOTES

NA GRUAGAICHEAN

LOCATION
Fort William

HEIGHT
1056 Metres
3464 Feet

DATE CLIMBED

ENJOYABLE
☆ ☆ ☆

ROUTE

CONDITION

NOTES

RUADH STAC MOR

LOCATION
Ullapool

HEIGHT
918 Metres
3011 Feet

DATE CLIMBED
_____

ENJOYABLE
☆ ☆ ☆

ROUTE
_____

CONDITION
_____

NOTES
_____
_____
_____

RUADH-STAC MOR (BEINN EIGHE)

LOCATION
Torridon

HEIGHT
1010 Metres
3313 Feet

DATE CLIMBED

ENJOYABLE
☆☆☆

ROUTE

CONDITION

NOTES

SAIL CHAORAINN

LOCATION
Kintail

HEIGHT
1002 Metres
3287 Feet

DATE CLIMBED

ENJOYABLE
☆ ☆ ☆

ROUTE

CONDITION

NOTES

SAILEAG

LOCATION

Kintail

HEIGHT

956 Metres
3136 Feet

DATE CLIMBED

_____

ENJOYABLE

☆ ☆ ☆

ROUTE

_____

CONDITION

_____

NOTES

_____
_____
_____

SCHIEHALLION

LOCATION **HEIGHT**
Perthshire   1083 Metres
              3553 Feet

DATE CLIMBED   **ENJOYABLE**

_____   ☆ ☆ ☆

ROUTE   **CONDITION**

_____   _____

NOTES

_____
_____
_____

SEANA BHRAIGH

LOCATION
Ullapool

HEIGHT
926 Metres
3038 Feet

DATE CLIMBED

ENJOYABLE
☆ ☆ ☆

ROUTE

CONDITION

NOTES

SGAIRNEACH MHOR

LOCATION
Cairngorms

HEIGHT
991 Metres
3251 Feet

DATE CLIMBED

_____

ENJOYABLE
☆ ☆ ☆

ROUTE

_____

CONDITION

_____

NOTES

_____

_____

_____

201

SGIATH CHUIL

LOCATION
Loch Lomond

HEIGHT
921 Metres
3021 Feet

DATE CLIMBED

ENJOYABLE
☆☆☆

ROUTE

CONDITION

NOTES

SGOR AN LOCHAIN UAINE

LOCATION

Cairngorms

HEIGHT

1258 Metres
4127 Feet

DATE CLIMBED

ENJOYABLE

☆ ☆ ☆

ROUTE

CONDITION

NOTES

SGOR GAIBHRE

LOCATION
Fort William

HEIGHT
955 Metres
3133 Feet

DATE CLIMBED

ENJOYABLE
☆ ☆ ☆

ROUTE

CONDITION

NOTES

SGOR GAOITH

LOCATION
Cairngorms

HEIGHT
1118 Metres
3667 Feet

DATE CLIMBED

ENJOYABLE
☆☆☆

ROUTE

CONDITION

NOTES

SGOR NA H-ULAIDH

LOCATION
Fort William

HEIGHT
994 Metres
3261 Feet

DATE CLIMBED

ENJOYABLE
☆ ☆ ☆

ROUTE

CONDITION

NOTES

SGORR DHEARG (BEINN A'BHEITHIR)

LOCATION
Fort William

HEIGHT
1024 Metres
3359 Feet

DATE CLIMBED

ENJOYABLE
☆☆☆

ROUTE

CONDITION

NOTES

SGORR DHONUILL (BEINN A'BHEITHIR)

LOCATION
Fort William

HEIGHT
1001 Metres
3284 Feet

DATE CLIMBED

ENJOYABLE
☆ ☆ ☆

ROUTE

CONDITION

NOTES

208

SGORR NAM FIANNAIDH (AONACH EAGACH)

LOCATION
Fort William

HEIGHT
967 Metres
3172 Feet

DATE CLIMBED

ENJOYABLE
☆ ☆ ☆

ROUTE

CONDITION

NOTES

SGORR RUADH

LOCATION

Torridon

HEIGHT

962 Metres
3156 Feet

DATE CLIMBED

☆ ☆ ☆

ENJOYABLE

ROUTE

CONDITION

NOTES

SGURR A'BHEALAICH DHEIRG

LOCATION
Kintail

HEIGHT
1036 Metres
3398 Feet

DATE CLIMBED

ENJOYABLE
☆ ☆ ☆

ROUTE

CONDITION

NOTES

SGURR A'CHAORACHAIN

LOCATION
Torridon

HEIGHT
1053 Metres
3454 Feet

DATE CLIMBED

ENJOYABLE
☆ ☆ ☆

ROUTE

CONDITION

NOTES

SGURR A'CHOIRE GHLAIS

LOCATION
Loch Ness

HEIGHT
1083 Metres
3553 Feet

DATE CLIMBED

ENJOYABLE
☆ ☆ ☆

ROUTE

CONDITION

NOTES

SGURR A'GHREADAIDH

LOCATION
Islands

HEIGHT
973 Metres
3192 Feet

DATE CLIMBED

ENJOYABLE
☆ ☆ ☆

ROUTE

CONDITION

NOTES

214

SGURR A'MHADAIDH

LOCATION
Islands

HEIGHT
918 Metres
3011 Feet

DATE CLIMBED

ENJOYABLE
☆ ☆ ☆

ROUTE

CONDITION

NOTES

SGURR A'MHAIM

LOCATION
Fort William

HEIGHT
1099 Metres
3605 Feet

DATE CLIMBED

ENJOYABLE
☆ ☆ ☆

ROUTE

CONDITION

NOTES

SGURR A'MHAORAICH

LOCATION
Fort William

HEIGHT
1027 Metres
3369 Feet

DATE CLIMBED

ENJOYABLE
☆ ☆ ☆

ROUTE

CONDITION

NOTES

SGURR ALASDAIR

LOCATION
Islands

HEIGHT
992 Metres
3254 Feet

DATE CLIMBED

ENJOYABLE
☆ ☆ ☆

ROUTE

CONDITION

NOTES

SGURR AN DOIRE LEATHAIN

LOCATION
Kintail

HEIGHT
1010 Metres
3313 Feet

DATE CLIMBED

ENJOYABLE
☆ ☆ ☆

ROUTE

CONDITION

NOTES

SGURR AN LOCHAIN

LOCATION
Kintail

HEIGHT
1004 Metres
3293 Feet

DATE CLIMBED

ENJOYABLE
☆ ☆ ☆

ROUTE

CONDITION

NOTES

SGURR BAN

LOCATION
Ullapool

HEIGHT
989 Metres
3244 Feet

DATE CLIMBED

ENJOYABLE
☆☆☆

ROUTE

CONDITION

NOTES

SGURR BREAC

LOCATION
Ullapool

HEIGHT
999 Metres
3277 Feet

DATE CLIMBED

ENJOYABLE
☆ ☆ ☆

ROUTE

CONDITION

NOTES

SGURR CHOINNICH

LOCATION
Torridon

HEIGHT
999 Metres
3277 Feet

DATE CLIMBED

ENJOYABLE
☆ ☆ ☆

ROUTE

CONDITION

NOTES

SGURR CHOINNICH MOR

LOCATION
Fort William

HEIGHT
1094 Metres
3589 Feet

DATE CLIMBED

ENJOYABLE
☆ ☆ ☆

ROUTE

CONDITION

NOTES

SGURR DUBH MOR

LOCATION
Islands

HEIGHT
944 Metres
3097 Feet

DATE CLIMBED

ENJOYABLE
☆ ☆ ☆

ROUTE

CONDITION

NOTES

SGURR EILDE MOR

LOCATION
Fort William

HEIGHT
1010 Metres
3313 Feet

DATE CLIMBED

ENJOYABLE
☆ ☆ ☆

ROUTE

CONDITION

NOTES

SGURR FHUAR-THUILL

LOCATION
Loch Ness

HEIGHT
1049 Metres
3441 Feet

DATE CLIMBED

ENJOYABLE
☆ ☆ ☆

ROUTE

CONDITION

NOTES

SGURR FHUARAN

LOCATION
Kintail

HEIGHT
1067 Metres
3500 Feet

DATE CLIMBED

ENJOYABLE
☆ ☆ ☆

ROUTE

CONDITION

NOTES

SGURR FIONA (AN TEALLACH)

LOCATION
Ullapool

HEIGHT
1060 Metres
3477 Feet

DATE CLIMBED

ENJOYABLE
☆☆☆

ROUTE

CONDITION

NOTES

SGURR MHIC CHOINNICH

LOCATION
Islands

HEIGHT
948 Metres
3110 Feet

DATE CLIMBED

ENJOYABLE
☆☆☆

ROUTE

CONDITION

NOTES

SGURR MOR

LOCATION
Ullapool

HEIGHT
1110 Metres
3641 Feet

DATE CLIMBED

ENJOYABLE
☆ ☆ ☆

ROUTE

CONDITION

NOTES

SGURR MOR (BEINN ALLIGIN)

LOCATION
Torridon

HEIGHT
986 Metres
3234 Feet

DATE CLIMBED

ENJOYABLE
☆☆☆

ROUTE

CONDITION

NOTES

SGURR MOR (LOCH QUOICH)

LOCATION
Fort William

HEIGHT
1003 Metres
3290 Feet

DATE CLIMBED

ENJOYABLE
☆ ☆ ☆

ROUTE

CONDITION

NOTES

SGURR NA BANACHDICH

LOCATION
Islands

HEIGHT
965 Metres
3166 Feet

DATE CLIMBED

ENJOYABLE
☆ ☆ ☆

ROUTE

CONDITION

NOTES

SGURR NA CARNACH

LOCATION
Kintail

HEIGHT
1002 Metres
3287 Feet

DATE CLIMBED

ENJOYABLE
☆ ☆ ☆

ROUTE

CONDITION

NOTES

SGURR NA CICHE

LOCATION

Fort William

HEIGHT

1040 Metres
3412 Feet

DATE CLIMBED

ENJOYABLE

☆ ☆ ☆

ROUTE

CONDITION

NOTES

236

SGURR NA CISTE DUIBHE

LOCATION
Kintail

HEIGHT
1027 Metres
3369 Feet

DATE CLIMBED

ENJOYABLE
☆ ☆ ☆

ROUTE

CONDITION

NOTES

SGURR NA LAPAICH

LOCATION
Loch Ness

HEIGHT
1150 Metres
3772 Feet

DATE CLIMBED

ENJOYABLE
☆ ☆ ☆

ROUTE

CONDITION

NOTES

SGURR NA RUAIDHE

LOCATION
Loch Ness

HEIGHT
993 Metres
3257 Feet

DATE CLIMBED

ENJOYABLE
☆ ☆ ☆

ROUTE

CONDITION

NOTES

239

SGURR NA SGINE

LOCATION
Kintail

HEIGHT
945 Metres
3100 Feet

DATE CLIMBED

ENJOYABLE
☆ ☆ ☆

ROUTE

CONDITION

NOTES

240

SGURR NAN CEATHREAMHNAN

LOCATION
Loch Ness

HEIGHT
1151 Metres
3776 Feet

DATE CLIMBED

ENJOYABLE
☆ ☆ ☆

ROUTE

CONDITION

NOTES

SGURR NAN CLACH GEALA

LOCATION
Ullapool

HEIGHT
1093 Metres
3585 Feet

DATE CLIMBED

ENJOYABLE
☆ ☆ ☆

ROUTE

CONDITION

NOTES

SGURR NAN COIREACHAN (GLEN DESSARY)

LOCATION
Fort William

HEIGHT
953 Metres
3126 Feet

DATE CLIMBED

ENJOYABLE
☆ ☆ ☆

ROUTE

CONDITION

NOTES

SGURR NAN COIREACHAN (GLENFINNAN)

LOCATION
Fort William

HEIGHT
956 Metres
3136 Feet

DATE CLIMBED
_____

ENJOYABLE
☆ ☆ ☆

ROUTE
_____

CONDITION
_____

NOTES
_____
_____
_____

SGURR NAN CONBHAIREAN

LOCATION
Kintail

HEIGHT
1109 Metres
3638 Feet

DATE CLIMBED

ENJOYABLE
☆ ☆ ☆

ROUTE

CONDITION

NOTES

SGURR NAN EACH

LOCATION
Ullapool

HEIGHT
923 Metres
3028 Feet

DATE CLIMBED

ENJOYABLE
☆ ☆ ☆

ROUTE

CONDITION

NOTES

SGURR NAN EAG

LOCATION
Islands

HEIGHT
924 Metres
3031 Feet

DATE CLIMBED
_____

ENJOYABLE
☆ ☆ ☆

ROUTE
_____

CONDITION
_____

NOTES
_____
_____
_____

SGURR NAN GILLEAN

LOCATION
Islands

HEIGHT
964 Metres
3162 Feet

DATE CLIMBED

ENJOYABLE
☆ ☆ ☆

ROUTE

CONDITION

NOTES

248

SGURR THUILM

LOCATION
Fort William

HEIGHT
963 Metres
3159 Feet

DATE CLIMBED

ENJOYABLE
☆ ☆ ☆

ROUTE

CONDITION

NOTES

SLIOCH

LOCATION

Torridon

HEIGHT

981 Metres
3218 Feet

DATE CLIMBED

ENJOYABLE

☆ ☆ ☆

ROUTE

CONDITION

NOTES

SPIDEAN A'CHOIRE LEITH (LIATHACH)

LOCATION

Torridon

HEIGHT

1055 Metres
3461 Feet

DATE CLIMBED

ENJOYABLE

☆ ☆ ☆

ROUTE

CONDITION

NOTES

SPIDEAN COIRE NAN CLACH (BEINN EIGHE)

LOCATION
Torridon

HEIGHT
993 Metres
3257 Feet

DATE CLIMBED

ENJOYABLE
☆ ☆ ☆

ROUTE

CONDITION

NOTES

SPIDEAN MIALACH

LOCATION
Fort William

HEIGHT
996 Metres
3267 Feet

DATE CLIMBED

ENJOYABLE
☆ ☆ ☆

ROUTE

CONDITION

NOTES

SRON A'CHOIRE GHAIRBH

LOCATION
Fort William

HEIGHT
937 Metres
3074 Feet

DATE CLIMBED

ENJOYABLE
☆ ☆ ☆

ROUTE

CONDITION

NOTES

STOB A'CHOIRE MHEADHOIN

LOCATION
Fort William

HEIGHT
1106 Metres
3628 Feet

DATE CLIMBED

ENJOYABLE
☆☆☆

ROUTE

CONDITION

NOTES

STOB A'CHOIRE ODHAIR

LOCATION
Argyll

HEIGHT
945 Metres
3100 Feet

DATE CLIMBED

ENJOYABLE
☆ ☆ ☆

ROUTE

CONDITION

NOTES

STOB BAN (GREY CORRIES)

LOCATION
Fort William

HEIGHT
977 Metres
3205 Feet

DATE CLIMBED

ENJOYABLE
☆ ☆ ☆

ROUTE

CONDITION

NOTES

STOB BAN (MAMORES)

LOCATION
Fort William

HEIGHT
999 Metres
3277 Feet

DATE CLIMBED

ENJOYABLE
☆ ☆ ☆

ROUTE

CONDITION

NOTES

STOB BINNEIN

LOCATION
Loch Lomond

HEIGHT
1165 Metres
3822 Feet

DATE CLIMBED

ENJOYABLE
☆ ☆ ☆

ROUTE

CONDITION

NOTES

STOB CHOIRE CLAURIGH

LOCATION
Fort William

HEIGHT
1177 Metres
3861 Feet

DATE CLIMBED

ENJOYABLE
☆ ☆ ☆

ROUTE

CONDITION

NOTES

STOB COIR AN ALBANNAICH

LOCATION
Fort William

HEIGHT
1044 Metres
3425 Feet

DATE CLIMBED

ENJOYABLE
☆☆☆

ROUTE

CONDITION

NOTES

STOB COIRE A'CHAIRN

LOCATION
Fort William

HEIGHT
981 Metres
3218 Feet

DATE CLIMBED
_____

ENJOYABLE
☆ ☆ ☆

ROUTE
_____

CONDITION
_____

NOTES
_____
_____
_____

STOB COIRE AN LAOIGH

LOCATION
Fort William

HEIGHT
1116 Metres
3661 Feet

DATE CLIMBED

ENJOYABLE
☆ ☆ ☆

ROUTE

CONDITION

NOTES

STOB COIRE EASAIN

LOCATION
Fort William

HEIGHT
1115 Metres
3658 Feet

DATE CLIMBED

ENJOYABLE
☆☆☆

ROUTE

CONDITION

NOTES

STOB COIRE RAINEACH (BUACHAILLE ETIVE BEAG)

LOCATION

Fort William

HEIGHT

925 Metres
3034 Feet

DATE CLIMBED

_____

ENJOYABLE

☆ ☆ ☆

ROUTE

_____

CONDITION

_____

NOTES

_____
_____
_____

STOB COIRE SGREAMHACH

LOCATION
Fort William

HEIGHT
1072 Metres
3517 Feet

DATE CLIMBED

ENJOYABLE
☆ ☆ ☆

ROUTE

CONDITION

NOTES

STOB COIRE SGRIODAIN

LOCATION
Fort William

HEIGHT
979 Metres
3211 Feet

DATE CLIMBED

ENJOYABLE
☆ ☆ ☆

ROUTE

CONDITION

NOTES

STOB DAIMH

LOCATION
Argyll

HEIGHT
998 Metres
3274 Feet

DATE CLIMBED

ENJOYABLE
☆ ☆ ☆

ROUTE

CONDITION

NOTES

STOB DEARG (BUACHAILLE ETIVE MOR)

LOCATION
Fort William

HEIGHT
1021 Metres
3349 Feet

DATE CLIMBED

ENJOYABLE
☆ ☆ ☆

ROUTE

CONDITION

NOTES

269

STOB DUBH (BUACHAILLE ETIVE BEAG)

LOCATION
Fort William

HEIGHT
956 Metres
3136 Feet

DATE CLIMBED

ENJOYABLE
☆ ☆ ☆

ROUTE

CONDITION

NOTES

STOB GHABHAR

LOCATION
Argyll

HEIGHT
1090 Metres
3576 Feet

DATE CLIMBED

ENJOYABLE
☆ ☆ ☆

ROUTE

CONDITION

NOTES

STOB NA BROIGE (BUACHAILLE ETIVE MOR)

LOCATION
Fort William

HEIGHT
956 Metres
3136 Feet

DATE CLIMBED

ENJOYABLE
☆ ☆ ☆

ROUTE

CONDITION

NOTES

STOB POITE COIRE ARDAIR

LOCATION
Fort William

HEIGHT
1054 Metres
3458 Feet

DATE CLIMBED

ENJOYABLE
☆ ☆ ☆

ROUTE

CONDITION

NOTES

STUC A'CHROIN

LOCATION

Perthshire

HEIGHT

975 Metres
3198 Feet

DATE CLIMBED

ENJOYABLE

☆ ☆ ☆

ROUTE

CONDITION

NOTES

STUCHD AN LOCHAIN

LOCATION
Perthshire

HEIGHT
960 Metres
3149 Feet

DATE CLIMBED

ENJOYABLE
☆ ☆ ☆

ROUTE

CONDITION

NOTES

THE CAIRNWELL

LOCATION
Cairngorms

HEIGHT
933 Metres
3061 Feet

DATE CLIMBED

ENJOYABLE
☆ ☆ ☆

ROUTE

CONDITION

NOTES

THE DEVIL'S POINT

LOCATION
Cairngorms

HEIGHT
1004 Metres
3293 Feet

DATE CLIMBED

ENJOYABLE
☆ ☆ ☆

ROUTE

CONDITION

NOTES

THE SADDLE

LOCATION
Kintail

HEIGHT
1010 Metres
3313 Feet

DATE CLIMBED

ENJOYABLE
☆ ☆ ☆

ROUTE

CONDITION

NOTES

TOLL CREAGACH

LOCATION
Loch Ness

HEIGHT
1054 Metres
3458 Feet

DATE CLIMBED
_____

ENJOYABLE
☆ ☆ ☆

ROUTE
_____

CONDITION
_____

NOTES

_____
_____
_____

TOLMOUNT

LOCATION
Cairngorms

HEIGHT
958 Metres
3143 Feet

DATE CLIMBED

ENJOYABLE
☆ ☆ ☆

ROUTE

CONDITION

NOTES

TOM A'CHOINICH

LOCATION
Loch Ness

HEIGHT
1113 Metres
3651 Feet

DATE CLIMBED

ENJOYABLE
☆☆☆

ROUTE

CONDITION

NOTES

TOM BUIDHE

LOCATION
Cairngorms

HEIGHT
957 Metres
3139 Feet

DATE CLIMBED

ENJOYABLE
☆ ☆ ☆

ROUTE

CONDITION

NOTES

TOM NA GRUAGAICH (BEINN ALLIGIN)

LOCATION

Torridon

HEIGHT

922 Metres
3024 Feet

DATE CLIMBED

ENJOYABLE

☆ ☆ ☆

ROUTE

CONDITION

NOTES

Printed in Great Britain
by Amazon